INTRODUCTION

Unlike American states or Swiss canton
not traditionally borne flags. The constit
states such as Germany and Brazil adopt flags as indications of
their authority, but British counties, which have never exercised
such powers as wielded by territories like the state of California
or Bavaria, have not required such expression. Certain territories
of the United Kingdom however, with differing historical, cultural
and linguistic legacies, have raised flags to mark themselves out as
distinct and different. A Cornish flag has existed since at least the
nineteenth century and is considered to be a 'national' flag reflecting
a status of the territory and its people as an assimilated Celtic land,
rather than just one amongst many English counties. Similarly, flags
for the North Atlantic archipelagos of Shetland and Orkney, with
strong Scandinavian heritages, were created in the twentieth century.
In recent years such enthusiasm has spread and many British shires
have marked their presence as distinct entities with a unique flag.
In much the same manner that one may wave a national flag to
demonstrate pride in one's nation or support for a national sports
team, so people wanting to demonstrate their local pride or indicate
their origins amongst a concert crowd or similar gathering have
turned to flags as a natural means of doing so.

There being no 'UK Flag Act' that might authorise such county
flags, no official method or process of establishing them operates,
but the UK's national flag charity, the Flag Institute, has established
a registry of designs adopted, which is recognised by government
and used as a reference in official circles, lending it a de facto official
status. The registry was established at the turn of the twenty-
first century as Devon adopted its flag, followed by Lincolnshire,
and these newly created designs joined several long-established,
traditional flags on the registry such as Essex, Cornwall and Shetland.
In recent years the adoption of county flags has markedly expanded,

with all thirty-nine counties of England now being represented on the registry. Seven of the thirteen Welsh counties are included, whilst Scotland still has a way to go, with only ten of its thirty-four shires present.

For inclusion in the registry, designs must be unique within the UK (i.e. no other UK area or organisation is using the design); be in the public domain (i.e. not subject to copyright); and represent a true, historic county, not a modern administrative area. Flags may be traditional – Cornwall's flag being such an example – selected by a public vote, or chosen by an appropriate county organisation. In Scotland, all flags must be sanctioned by the heraldic authority, the Office of the Lord Lyon.

In practice a county flag has been added to the registry upon endorsement by either a local authority representing the area – the county flag of Hertfordshire, for example, was registered after its sanction by Hertfordshire County Council – or an official such as a Lord Lieutenant or High Sherrif of a county – the flags of Berkshire and Bedfordshire being endorsed by these respective officials. County flags have also been established by the efforts of local interest groups, for example the flag of Lancashire appeared as a result of a request from the Friends of Real Lancashire. In some cases, these criteria have been met with designs specifically produced as the result of a competition; others are long-standing local symbols used by county authorities and county-based organisations which are deployed as flags, such as the flag of Warwickshire.

Since 2019, following efforts by the author, the registered county flags have flown on Parliament Square, Westminster, each summer, in the days surrounding 23 July, which has been recognised by government as County Flags Day. This occasion was originally devised by Brady Ells in 2014, and chosen in recognition of the date being when Devon's flag was registered, which initiated the modern practice of flag adoption by most counties.

Thanks are due to Owain Vaughan for supplying the county map and to Brady Ells for his significant research contribution to this work and for supplying the cover photograph of the county flags displayed at Parliament Square.

COUNTY FLAGS OF ENGLAND, SCOTLAND AND WALES

JASON SABER

AMBERLEY

This edition first published 2024

Amberley Publishing
The Hill, Stroud
Gloucestershire GL5 4EP

www.amberley-books.com

British Library Cataloguing in Publication Data.
A catalogue record for this book is available from the British Library.

ISBN 978 1 3981 2008 2 (print)
ISBN 978 1 3981 2009 9 (ebook)

Typesetting by SJmagic DESIGN SERVICES, India.
Printed in Great Britain.

CONTENTS

County Flags Day 2015.

Brady Ells with the Northamptonshire flag.

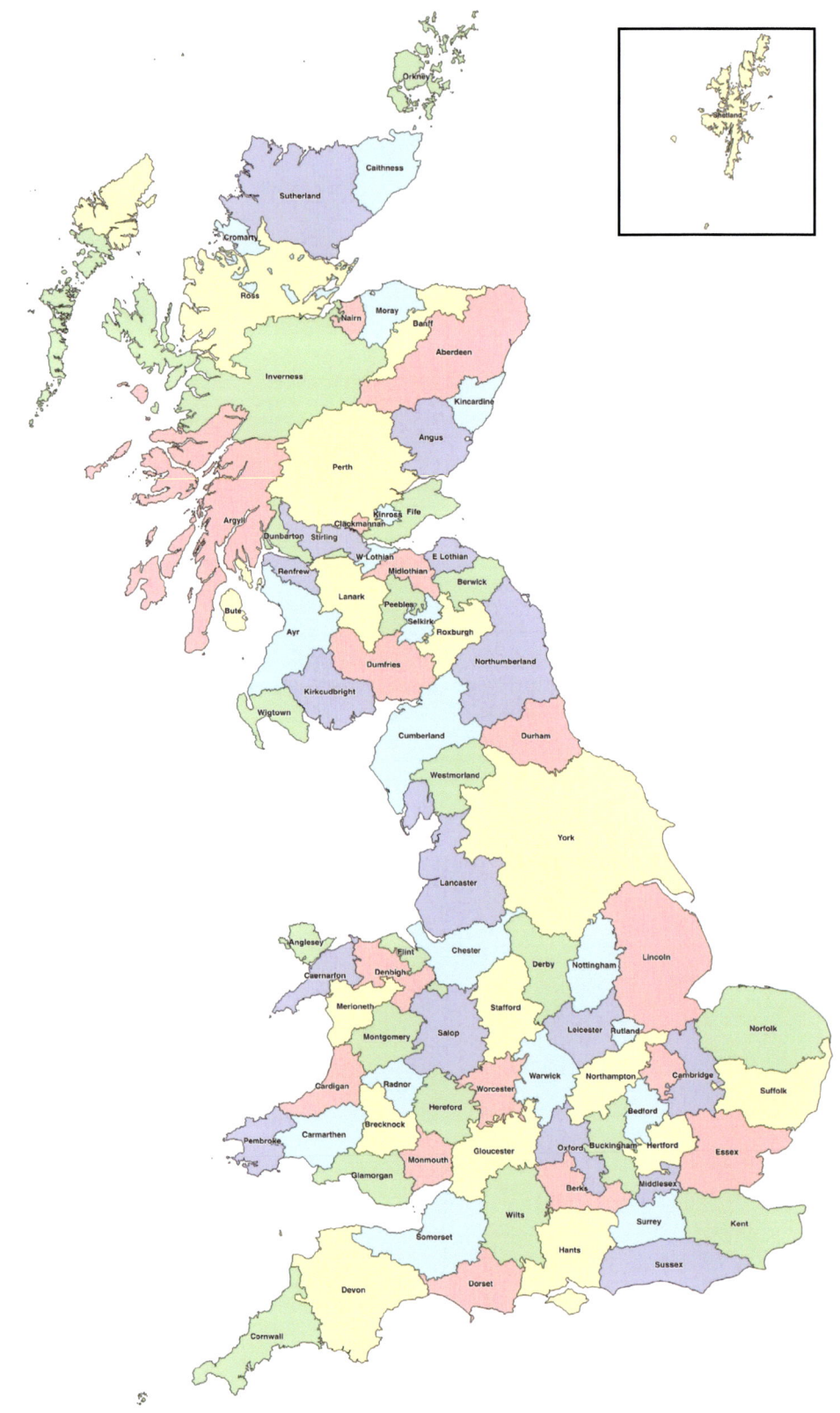

ENGLAND

Kent, Sussex, Hampshire and Dorset.

Bedfordshire

Bedfordshire's flag was registered on 11 September 2014, following a campaign led by county native Luke Blackstaffe, with support from Bedfordshire High Sherrif, Colin Osbourne. The design is a slightly modified version of the arms used by the former Bedfordshire County Council, which was abolished on 1 April 2009. The design combines three escallops or shells on a black field, from the arms of the Russells, Dukes of Bedford, while the red and yellow (gold) quarters derive from the arms of the Beauchamps, a leading family in the county after the Norman Conquest who constructed Bedford Castle. The blue and white wavy stripes are a reference to the River Ouse which flows through the county and are a traditional heraldic pattern for any water feature. The design is much used across the county by many sporting and other organisations, making it the obvious choice for the county's flag.

The flag of Bedfordshire flying in the county.

Berkshire

Berkshire's flag was registered on 27 February 2017 following declarations of support from twenty-four local organisations, backed by the county's Lord Lieutenant, James Puxley. The flag features the traditional hart (stag) and oak theme associated with the county for several centuries, which appears on the badges, emblems and logos of a large number of county organisations. The hart and oak refer generally to the forestlands of Berkshire and specifically to the legend of a late fourteenth-century royal huntsman named Herne the Hunter. Legend has it that after various nefarious deeds by his jealous rivals, this one-time favourite of the king was dismissed from royal service. Distraught, he hanged himself from an oak tree which was then struck by lightning. The hart is 'one of the manifestations of his restless spirit' and, according to Michael Drayton's 1627 poem, a banner depicting such a scene was carried by the men of Berkshire at the Battle of Agincourt: 'Barkshire a Stag, under an Oake that stood.' The colours of the flag are those used in a seal by the former Berkshire County Council. Following its registration the flag was officially raised at the Berkshire County Show, Newbury, on 17 September 2017.

Raising of the Berkshire flag.

Buckinghamshire

Buckinghamshire's flag was registered on 20 May 2011. A traditional design long associated with the county, where waterfowl such as swans are endemic, the bird was repeatedly used as a family badge, seal or on arms by local nobles across the centuries and ultimately adopted, along with the red and black livery colours of the Stafford family, who had been Dukes of Buckingham, for civic use by the county town of Buckingham. The design appears on John Speed's 1610 county map of Buckinghamshire and was described seventeen years later by the poet Michael Drayton in his 1627 work the 'Ballad of Agincourt' where he wrote, 'The mustred men for Buckingham, are gone Under the Swan, the Armes of that olde Towne.' With this long-standing pedigree the design was sufficiently familiar for inclusion in the arms awarded to the county council in 1948 and thereafter for recognition as the county flag.

Cambridgeshire

The flags of Lincolnshire, Cambridgeshire and Northamptonshire at the point where the three shires meet.

The flag of Cambridgeshire.

The Cambridgeshire flag was created by Brady Ells and registered on 1 February 2015, the day it was announced as the winning design in a competition held to select a flag for the county. The competition, endorsed by several local authorities, ran throughout 2014. This winning design was one of six finalists selected from the original submissions and put to a public vote. The three gold crowns are the arms of the kingdom of East Anglia, in which Cambridgeshire is located. The three crowns flank two wavy lines in the light blue colours of Cambridge University, representing the River Cam which flows through the county.

Cheshire

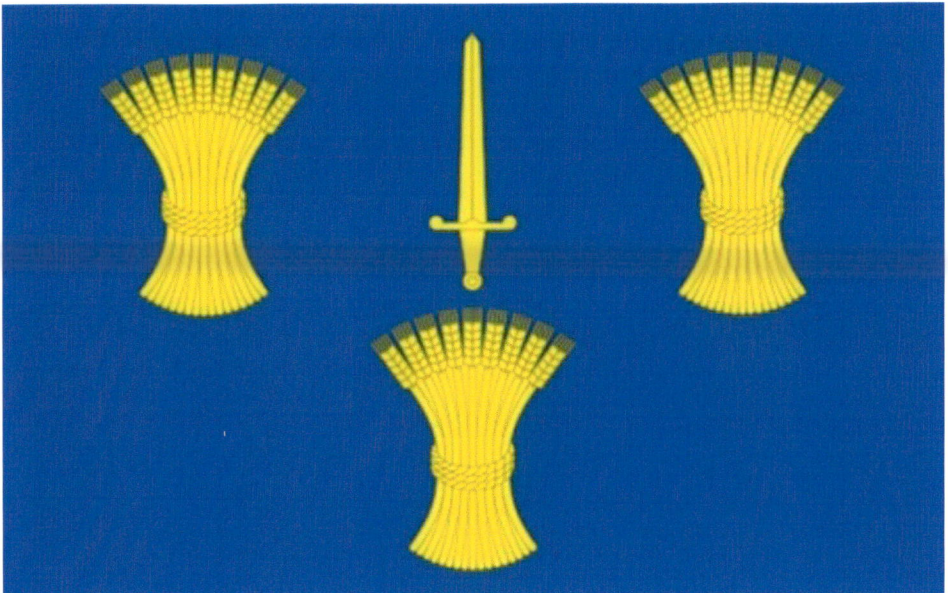

Three gold wheatsheaves, known heraldically as garbs, on a blue background have been associated with either the Earldom of Cheshire, the county of Cheshire or its county town, Chester, for several centuries. The Earldom of Cheshire was originally created by William I (1028–87). Its sixth earl, Ranulf de Blondeville (1170–1232), was the first to use the three garbs. These were deployed several centuries later, as the arms of the city of Chester in 1560, although by this time they had acquired a sword between them. Tradition holds that the addition of the sword reflects the description that the Earl of Chester held the lands of the County Palatinate (meaning of the palace and indicating a measure of autonomy) 'as freely by his sword as the King of England held by his crown', although it is not precisely clear when or under what circumstance this addition was effected. The garbs and sword are much used by county bodies and with its trenchant history the design was the obvious choice for registration as the county flag, which occurred on 10 April 2013 after expressions of support from a number of countywide bodies.

Cornwall

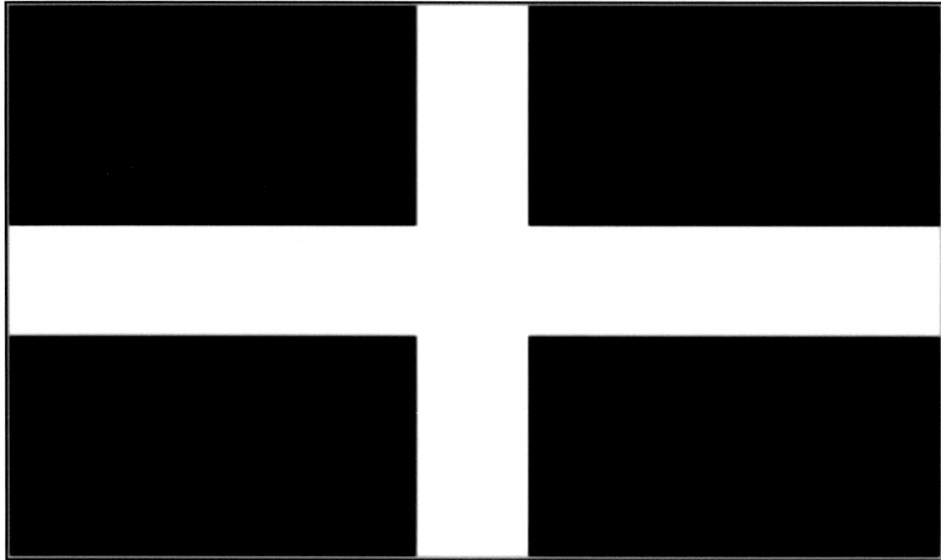

Cornwall's flag, the Cross of Saint Piran or Saint Piran's flag, is one of the oldest designs in the British Isles. The first definitive reference to it is in an 1838 work entitled *The Parochial History of Cornwall* by Davies Gilbert, in which he writes 'a white cross on a black ground (that) was formerly the banner of St Perran and the Standard of Cornwall; probably with some allusion to the black ore and the white metal of tin', but it is believed that the design may date at least from the medieval period. As indicated, the black base colour of the flag is believed to symbolise the colours of black Cornish ore and the white of the cross, the tin which emerges from it when heated. Legend holds that the flag reflects the discovery of tin in the territory by the sixth-century abbot Saint Piran, who adopted the contrasting colours upon seeing the white molten tin spilling out of the black ore in his fire. He is accordingly recognised both as the patron saint of tin miners generally and of Cornwall particularly. With a firm sense of Celtic heritage, many residents regard the flag of Cornwall as a symbol of nationhood, comparable to the red dragon of Wales and Saint Andrew's Cross of Scotland and it is consequently much used to represent Cornish identity.

County Durham

The County Durham flag was the winner of a 2013 competition established by adventurer and campaigner Andy Strangeway, in cooperation with the Durham County Council. Registered on 21 November, the flag was created by James Moffat and his twin daughters Katie and Holly, from Chilton in the county, and was one of six finalists in the competition, selected by a judging panel for a public vote. The flag features the locally familiar Saint Cuthbert's Cross, in a counter-changed blue and yellow design, these colours having appeared in the arms and symbols of various authorities and bodies that have administered County Durham through the ages.

Cuthbert was a monk, born in the kingdom of Northumbria, associated with the monasteries of Melrose and Lindisfarne in the kingdom. After his death he became one of the most important medieval saints of England, with a cult centred at Durham Cathedral, where his remains were eventually interred and he is generally regarded as the patron saint of northern England. When his coffin was last inspected on 17 May 1827, a typical Anglo-Saxon square pectoral (worn on the chest) cross of gold, with splayed ends and studded with garnets, was discovered, buried amongst the robes on the body. The pectoral cross's firm association with the county was notably demonstrated by its use by the county scout movement in the 1930s and has become a common local theme.

Cumberland

The Cumberland flag is derived from the arms of the former Cumberland County Council. It was registered on 13 December 2012. The blue and white wavy lines symbolise the famous lakes of the county and its coastline, whilst the green upper half with grass-of-Parnassus flowers recalls its marshy uplands and fertile plains. The design was already in popular general use as flag to represent the county and featured on the badges of local sports clubs. Registration was completed after support for the proposed flag was received from over a dozen county associations.

Derbyshire

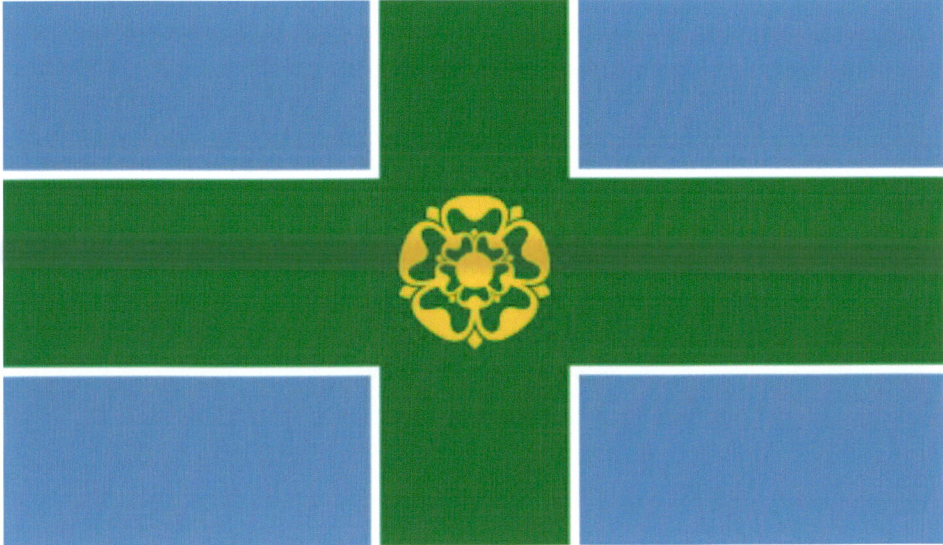

The flag of Derbyshire was registered on 16 September 2008. It was designed by Martin Enright of Derby and was the winning entry in a competition organised by BBC Radio presenter Andy Whittaker, after his audience enquired about establishing something in Derbyshire comparable to the much-loved Saint Piran's flag in Cornwall and the local pride it conveys. A campaign was duly launched to create one. A number of submissions were received, which were then whittled down by a specially convened panel to a shortlist of three for a public vote. This process involved lots of feedback from people outlining what they hoped to see in a county flag, which led to the development of the three contenders after several ideas had been merged and perfected. The winning design has a light blue background, this shade being described as one of the traditional colours of the county, as worn, for example, by the county cricket team for One-Day and 20/20 competitions and is also seen as representative of the county's rivers and reservoirs. Over the light blue shade is a green cross with a thin white border (fimbriation), which symbolises Derbyshire's lush, verdant countryside and the cross itself highlights Derbyshire's location at the centre of the country. At the centre of the cross is a Tudor rose, used as an emblem of Derbyshire since the fifteenth century and found on the arms of the county council and the insignia of several Derbyshire organisations, including the county cricket club, whose golden colour is the inspiration for the rose on the flag. This hue also serves to distinguish the rose from the several rose depictions found on other county flags.

Devon

Devon's flag, dedicated to Saint Petroc, was registered on 23 July 2003. The colours of the flag are those popularly identified with the county, appearing on the shirts of its Rugby Union team, Exeter University sports teams, Plymouth Argyle football club and used in the early twentieth century by Exeter City football club. Viscount Exmouth also flew a dark green flag with white circles at the Bombardment of Algiers in 1816. The colours are specifically taken to represent the county's rolling lush hills and the high windswept moors of Dartmoor and Exmoor, while the white represents both the salt spray of Devon's two coastlines and the china clay industry. The flag, created by student Ryan Sealey, was the winning entry in a competition initiated by BBC Radio Devon, inspired by the popularity of the flag of neighbouring Cornwall, with many Devonians feeling that their county was in need of an easily

The flag of Devon unfurled at Glastonbury music festival.

recognised icon to help promote county products and tourism. This led to a shortlist of a dozen designs and a web-based poll to select the county flag from amongst them. Most of the designs featured the combination of black, white and green and the theme of a black-edged cross appeared six times amongst the shortlisted proposals, differing only by the degree of thickness of the black edging of the white cross. The winning version topped the first poll by a narrow margin and then won a second vote, held to remove any doubt.

Dorset

Dorset's vibrant flag was registered on 16 September 2008 as the winner of a competition. This followed a campaign to see the design adopted on the basis of popular use and appeal. In the wake of its burgeoning popularity, the local council organised a county flag competition, which the flag duly won by an overwhelming majority. Unlike most counties, Dorset was not associated with a distinct emblem but in 2006, following the adoption of a flag by neighbouring Devon, Dave White of Dorchester engaged with Dorset expatriate Stephen Coombs to create something comparable for their county. With an interest in heraldry, Stephen sought a

The flags of Hampshire and Dorset at their boundary at the beach by Bournemouth.

simple flag that was easily recognised and drawn, and conscious of the cross-themed flags borne by Dorset's neighbours and adopted by Lincolnshire, he opted for the same cross pattern which he felt had become something of a standard for English county flags. He took the red and white colours of Dorset County Council's arms and recognising that red, gold (yellow) and white was a colour combination rarely seen on flags, proposed a golden yellow flag with a white cross, edged (in heraldic terms 'fimbriated') in red. Dave White created the first illustration of this idea, prompting discussion and eventual agreement between the two, regarding the proportions of the cross and its edging and encouraged by flag enthusiast Jason Saber, he then promoted the design, spearheading the successful campaign for its adoption as the county flag. Dorset's flag is most distinctive with a unique and meaningful colour combination, as 'Golden Cap' is the name of the highest point on the county's famed Jurassic Coast, while 'Gold Hill' in Shaftesbury is a famous location, often featured in television productions.

Essex

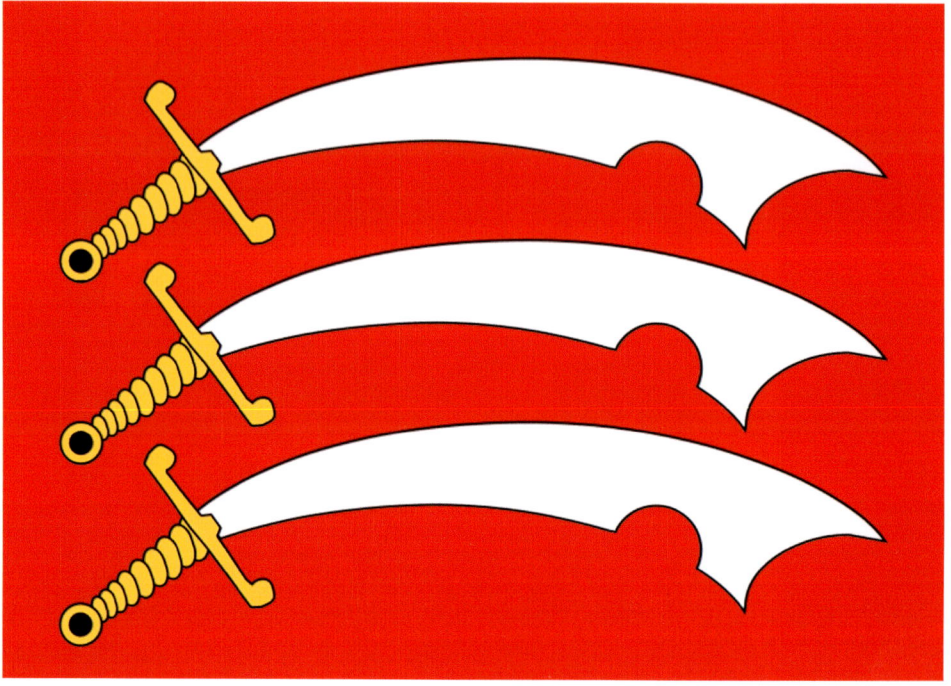

Three white seaxes (short Saxon swords) with gold pommels on a red field were the arms ascribed to the ancient kingdom of the East Saxons, or Essex, by Richard Verstegen in his 1605 work *A Restitution of Decayed Intelligence*, where he stated that 'Erkenwyne king of the East-Saxons did beare for his armes, three [seaxes] argent, in a field gules', i.e. three white, short Saxon swords on a red background. John Speed subsequently included the arms in his 1611 atlas *The Theatre of the Empire of Great Britaine*, where they appear on the title page of the work and twice on a map of the Anglo-Saxon heptarchy, the seven kingdoms of that era. It is believed that the name of the Saxons was itself derived from the Seax, the form of weapon for which they were best known, so it is logical that the weapons might be chosen as a reflection of the name. Historian James Lloyd has proposed two theories based on a medieval description of arms attributed to the seven kingdoms, where, remarkably, the arms for the Kingdom of Kent depict three seaxes, white on a red background!

Plausibly, the seaxes may simply be intended as a visual reference to the name of the people who bear them, the Saxons, the name being commonly applied to all Germanic settlers of Britain. A more gruesome suggestion is that they specifically recall the infamous 'Night of the Long Knives', when, at a negotiation with the Britons, the cry 'Take out your seaxes!' was issued by the chieftain Hengest, as a signal for a treacherous attack. Extensive study of Kent's white horse emblem indicates that Richard Verstegan, in his above work, later assigned the white horse to Kent on the basis of prevailing ideas and re-assigned the above three seaxes emblem to Essex, based on the etymological link between the name of that kingdom and the seaxes depicted. The seaxes of the Kingdom of Essex then appeared in an account of the Anglo-Saxon Heptarchy 'Divi Britannici' by Sir Winston Churchill (direct ancestor of the famous twentieth-century one), published in 1675, and have subsequently been regarded as the emblem of the kingdom, turned county, of Essex for centuries. They can be found in Westminster Abbey, a reference to the belief that King Sebert of Essex founded a church on the site in 604 and in 1770 Peter Muilman published the first volume of his History of Essex with a female figure depicted on the front, a shield by her side bearing the three seaxes. They later appeared on the masthead of the Chelmsford Chronicle, in 1815; were used on its fire plate by The Essex Equitable Insurance Society, established in Colchester in 1802; and were included on a print of Braintree Market in 1826. With this long association and usage, the banner of the attributed arms of Erkenwyn, his arms in flag form, was duly recognised as the Essex county flag, when the registry was first established in the early twenty-first century.

Gloucestershire

Gloucestershire's flag, registered in March 2008, was the winning entry in a competition held by the High Sheriff of the county, Jonathon Carr, to commemorate a millennium of the county's existence. It was designed by Jeremy Bentall from Hucclecote in the county, who described the flag thus: 'The green is representative of our rural county, the blue, the River Severn and the yellow, Cotswold Stone.' The cross design, a popular pattern for English county flags, features distinct shades: the base colour is 'apple green' and the edging of the blue cross (fimbriation) is 'cream'. In inviting entries, the Sheriff had stated that 'Several counties, especially in the West of the country, now have their own flags and I think the Millennium presents a good opportunity for Gloucestershire to have one of its own.'

The final decision was made by Mr Carr with the help of his wife Daphne. The flag was officially launched in a ceremony at Shire Hall, Gloucester.

The flag of Gloucestershire with Gloucester Cathedral.

Hampshire

The flag of Hampshire, conceived by Jason Saber and further refined by Brady Ells, retains the rose and crown pattern used in the county for several centuries, and was registered on 12 March 2019. The county has a strong association with the emblem of a rose: in the Great Hall in Winchester a round medieval table with a double Tudor rose of inner white petals and outer red ones at its centre is positioned on a wall, recalling the round table of Arthurian legend. It is believed that the powerful symbolism of the legendary round table promoted a strong association between the rose emblem and the county, with the description 'Hampshire Rose' being common and roses appearing in the arms used in many Hampshire towns. King Henry III (1216–72) adopted his own golden rose badge from his wife, Eleanor of Provence, and this was subsequently used by several English monarchs. Edmund, the first Duke of Lancaster (1341–1402), is believed to have distinguished his own badge by changing his father's golden rose to a red one. In 1283 he brought Somborne Hundred in Hampshire into the Earldom of Lancaster, establishing a connection between his own red rose and the county. The combined rose and crown emblem is likely to have originated when Henry IV (1399–1413) converted the

Duchy of Lancaster into an appendage of the Crown, as the personal fief of the reigning monarch, in 1399, symbolised by the addition of a crown to the rose emblem. This combination then appeared on the fourteenth-century staple seal in Southampton, the port being one of several designated for the import and export of specific 'staple' goods. A combined Rose and Crown was also the seal of the Keeper of the Records for Hampshire during the reign of Charles I. The oldest reference of a crown and rose in combination as a specific Hampshire emblem appears to date from 1681, with its inclusion as a decorative element on the ceremonial mace used by the Borough of Stockbridge and the 1686 mace used in the Borough of Petersfield. In the following centuries, the combination was included on locally issued currency and in 1842 a device comprising the rose surmounted by a crown, with a cap, surrounded by a wreath of laurel leaves, appeared on official documents. In 1889 Hampshire County Council was established and in 1895 it adopted this recognised county emblem of combined rose and crown as a heraldic badge (similar to a company logo), although without legal sanction.

This usage was formalised in 1992 with the award of official arms featuring a golden crown and a double rose with inner white detail, reflective of the rose on the table in the Great Hall in Winchester and other early depictions. The gold crown and red rose were placed against contrasting respective red and gold fields to enhance their visibility. These arms, as a banner, were then popularly, albeit unlawfully, used to represent the county generally, as the arms were solely the property of the council and the specific depiction of a Royal Crown was itself also strictly limited. Realising that such a pattern was ineligible for registration as the Hampshire flag, Jason Saber proposed substituting the form of a crown with a Saxon-style crown, which was free of any restrictions and a reference to the county's association with the era of Alfred the Great and his capital of Winchester, a suggestion enthusiastically accepted by Hampshire County Council and the county's Lord Lieutenant, Nigel Atkinson, who duly first raised the flag in an official capacity on the inaugural Hampshire Day, 15 July 2019, the date being the feast day of local saint Swithun (Swithin), often considered to be the county's patron saint.

Herefordshire

The Herefordshire flag, designed by Jason Saber, was the winner of a 2019 county flag competition, revealed at a ceremony at Hereford Cathedral on 2 November and duly added to the registry. The original design of the flag

was amended by the competition organisers upon its inclusion in the competition. The design, one of five finalists selected for public

vote, reworks the more distinctive elements found in the coat of arms awarded to Herefordshire County Council in 1946, namely, the base colour, the depiction of the River Wye and the depiction of a bull, of the Hereford breed. The basic colour of the flag is red, to reflect the famed red earth of the county but is a considerably darker shade than that found in the council arms, to emphasise the distinctive dark rich soil that is so typical of Herefordshire terrain. A bull's head, from the county's famous Hereford breed, features as the main element of the flag. The Hereford bull is a typical county theme, with a long pedigree of use; it has, for example, appeared on locally issued currency in the eighteenth century and been widely deployed on the insignia of Herefordshire organisations. A statue of a Hereford bull also stands in Hereford. At the base of the flag, three wavy stripes, white and blue, represent the River Wye which flows through the county. The three elements of dark red field, Herefordshire bull and River Wye are felt to be a concise graphic expression of the county.

Hertfordshire

Hertfordshire's flag was registered on 19 November 2008. The flag is a banner of the arms of the county council, released for public use following enquiries from members of the Flag Institute. In 2004 the organisers of the Hertfordshire County Show arranged a 'Parade of Flags' event as part of the proceedings but the event organiser, Mr Richard Walduck, expressed some surprise that the county itself appeared not to have a flag: 'I am absolutely amazed that Hertfordshire does not have its own flag. We would welcome ideas and support from Hertfordshire residents and businesses to help design and produce a Hertfordshire flag to lead the Parade of Flags event at next year's Herts County Show.' Unfortunately, this initial interest failed to produce a flag for the county; by 2008 with no flag appearing, flag enthusiast Jason Saber contacted fellow interested parties, including a resident of the county, to see if the situation might be remedied. A few ideas were produced and contact made with the local council, as a result of which the body decided that the preferred option would be to release its banner of arms for use as the county flag. Hertfordshire County Council, under the leadership of Robert Gordon, passed a resolution on 19 November 2008: 'This Council has, for the better representation of the County of Hertfordshire and its people, decided that the banner of the county council's arms, namely "Barry wavy of eight Azure and Argent an Inescutcheon Or charged with a Hart lodged proper" is a fitting and proper emblem for the county and its people and will from this day be the County flag of Hertfordshire.' The arms from which the flag is formed were awarded to the council on 3 June 1925. The blue and white waves are held to represent the many rivers of the county and the shield bearing a hart (stag) is taken from the arms of the Borough of Hertford, the county town. This depiction of a hart and a ford is thus a reference to the name of the town and the shire within which it sits. The gold colour of the shield was likely chosen as providing the best visibility. A representation of a hart is used by many different Hertfordshire bodies – often as a stylised logo – including its police and fire services.

Huntingdonshire

The Huntingdonshire flag was registered in 2009 following an enthusiastic campaign by The Huntingdonshire Society, at whose request it was eventually registered. Having established 25 April, the birthday of Oliver Cromwell, as 'Huntingdonshire Day' in 2002, registration of a county flag was a natural next step and promotion of the design began in 2007. Whilst several county flags are armorial banners formed from the patterns on the shield in a coat of arms, or are in part derived from or based on them, the Huntingdonshire flag was originally held aloft by a red lion, as a crest on the arms of Huntingdonshire council, awarded in 1937. Such usage of a flag as a decorative feature in a coat of arms is relatively unusual and the design was wholly appropriate for deployment as the county flag – it seemed all but designed with this very purpose in mind! The symbolism of the green flag, bearing a gold-ribboned hunting horn to symbolise Huntingdonshire, is apparent. Rupert Barnes, Secretary of the Huntingdonshire Society explained, 'The derivation of the hunting horn motif is obvious. It is found elsewhere too. The seal of Huntingdon has a huntsman holding a horn.' The same theme had also been present in the civic heraldry of several county towns and used by county-based organisations.

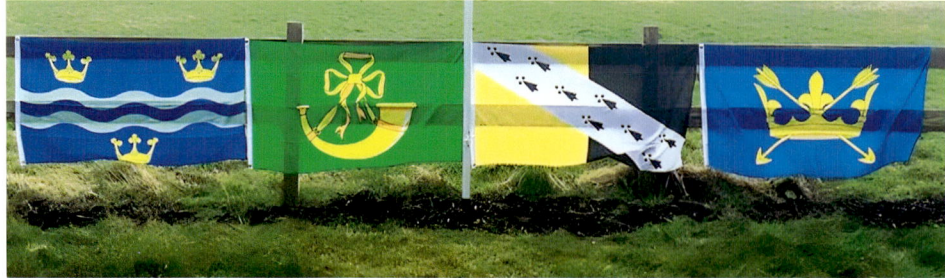

Flags of East Anglian neighbours Cambridgeshire, Huntingdonshire, Suffolk and Norfolk.

Kent

The flag of Kent is generally held to be one of the longest-established county emblems in Great Britain. It certainly has a pedigree of several centuries. The depiction of the flag on the registry is particularly flamboyant; a more traditional depiction

is also commonly seen. One school of thought postulates that the white horse of Kent derives from the ancient white horses cut into chalk downs and stamped on the coins of pre-Roman British kings. Another firm tradition holds that the emblem was borne aloft by fifth-century Jutish mercenaries, led on to the Kent shore by brothers Hengist and Horsa. There is, however, nothing to substantiate this claim, albeit that the names of the legendary siblings meant, respectively, stallion and horse.

The white horse emblem was first recorded in print in the 1605 work *A Restitution of Decayed Intelligence* by Richard Verstegen, which included an engraving of Hengist and Horsa landing in Kent in 449 under the banner of a rampant white horse. Although an appealing notion, the idea has been firmly disproved by historian James Lloyd in his 2017 work *The Saxon Steed and the White Horse of Kent*, volume 138 of *Archaeologia Cantiana*, the journal of the Kent Archaeological Society. Lloyd reveals that the Saxon Steed motif was an anachronistic promotion in fourteenth-century Germany that sought to establish linkage with the Germanic peoples of the fifth, based on historical descriptions of Hengest and Horsa found in the ninth-century work of the Venerable Bede, as part of an effort to promote the venerable status of German nobility in political competition. A German duke thus adopted a running horse for his arms, as a visual reference to the equine names of celebrated historical figures, with claims subsequently made that the arms had been passed down from ancient times to the current duke. The horse arms were thereafter embraced by all branches of the family and became a common regional theme. By this analysis it appears that Verstegen, who had moved to the continent, became acquainted with the myth that leaders in Saxony used equine arms inherited from their forbears and that the same set of emblems had been taken by their kinsmen on their migration to Kent. Before his account no such association is apparent but following Verstegen, John Speed included the white horse on the title page of his 1611 *Atlas of Great Britaine* to represent the kingdom of Kent and it then featured as the emblem of the Kingdom of Kent in *Divi Britannici* by Sir Winston Churchill (direct ancestor of the famous twentieth-century one), published in 1675. By the eighteenth century, the Saxon Steed which had been adopted by the House of Welf in the fourteenth century, was included in the arms of the Elector of Hanover and in 1714, Georg Ludwig from this dynasty acceded to the British throne as George I and upon his enthronement the British royal coat of arms was altered to accommodate his Hanoverian arms, including the 'Saxon Steed'. It then appeared on the masthead of the county newspaper, the *Kentish Post*, which first featured it in 1722, eight years after the German monarch's accession, definitively marking the rampant white stallion as a symbol of the county of Kent.

A Royal Warrant issued by George II, in 1751, ordered the display of the Hanoverian white horse on military caps and equipment.

Kent, Sussex and Surrey at the point where the three shires meet.

This order applied to the military as a whole but was markedly evident in the insignia of Kent regiments. Lloyd suggests that George I's accession to the British monarchy was not universally popular but this Protestant monarch was welcomed in Kent, which had a strong Protestant tradition. There was also an obvious similarity between the attributed arms of Hengest, founder of Kent, and those of the House of Hanover. In the words of James Lloyd, 'By purportedly reviving a symbol so clearly related to George I's ancestral arms, the Men of Kent advertised the ancient links between their county and his homeland and, more importantly, flaunted their Protestant credentials and their support for the Protestant king.'

In the following centuries the emblem has been much used by Kent organisations, cultural and sporting bodies such as Kent Cricket Club, and county-based companies, and formally awarded for its arms to Kent County Council in 1933. With its firm historical association and widespread usage, the rearing white stallion on red background was naturally recognised as the county flag of Kent and included on the registry from its inception.

Lancashire

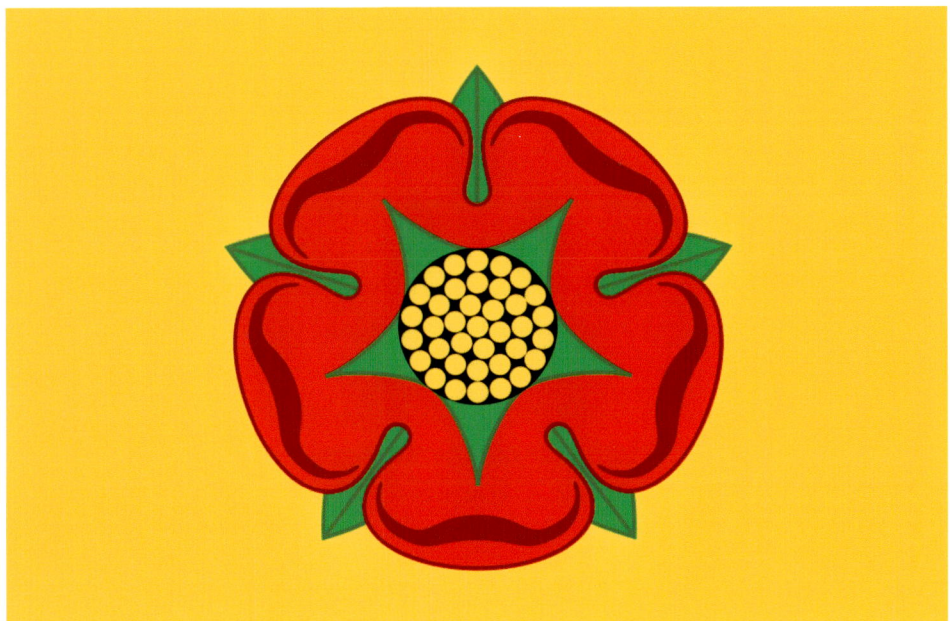

Lancashire's flag was registered in 2008. It features the county's traditional red rose with which it has long been associated. A rose had first been used as a royal badge by Henry III (r. 1216–72) who adopted his golden rose from his wife, Eleanor of Provence. This royal badge was then used by the four subsequent monarchs but Henry's son Edmund (Crouchback; 1245–96) the first Duke of Lancaster, distinguished his own badge by making the rose red. His descendants, the Dukes of Lancaster, used the badge as an emblem of the House of Lancaster. The specific variety or species of rose depicted is generally held to be the 'Rosa Gallica Officinalis', possibly the first cultivated rose. There are conflicting opinions regarding the prominence of the red rose during the period of the civil war, subsequently named the 'Wars of the Roses'. Although a badge of the House of Lancaster, it is conceivable that it came to prominence only with the victory of Henry VII (Tudor) at the Battle of Bosworth in 1485, in response to the white rose badge used by the rival House of York. This battle is depicted in an illustration by engraver and artist Charles Grignon (1721–1810) found in William Henry Montague's *History of England* published *c.* 1780. Remarkably, not only are the opposing factions shown with their respective rose emblems, but both are clearly deployed as flags! The term 'Wars of the Roses' is believed to have been first used in the novel *Anne of Geierstein* by Walter Scott in 1829, who is thought to have coined the term from the fictional scene in William Shakespeare's play *Henry VI Part 1*, where the opposing sides pick their different-coloured roses at the Temple Church. Perhaps the artist drew inspiration from the Shakespearean scene?

The promulgation of this Lancastrian badge allowed Henry Tudor to symbolise the restoration of peace and unity by creating the combined red and white Tudor rose that came to symbolise England as a whole. In the nineteenth century the red rose appeared as the badge, or on the banners, of several county militia regiments including the Royal Lancashire Militia and towards the end of the century it was also adopted by Lancashire County Cricket Club, demonstrating that the symbol had become firmly established as the county emblem. A cobblestone mosaic of the red rose was placed outside Manchester Town Hall, completed in 1877, and another in Williamson Park,

Lancaster. The red rose was entrenched as the county symbol during the First World War, when The 55th (West Lancashire) Territorial Division wore it on their shoulder flashes as their Divisional Sign and had the motto 'They win or die, who wear the Rose of Lancaster'. An official coat of arms was granted to Lancashire County Council in 1903 which featured several red roses against a golden background. During the twentieth century the red rose, against a white background, began to be flown informally by county residents as a flag. The Friends of Real Lancashire, seeking to register the design as the county flag, were advised that the white field could not be used as it already existed as a set of arms elsewhere but that use of the yellow base colour from the council arms was an option. This design, for which there were several local precedents, was duly registered.

The flag of Lancashire.

Leicestershire

The Leicestershire flag, created by vexillographer (flag designer) Jason Saber in 2011, was registered on 16 July 2021. The original design of the flag

which was widely flown prior to registration, continues to be seen. The flag uses the red and white colour scheme and zigzag pattern present in the shield of Leicestershire County Council, taken from the arms borne by local noble Simon de Montfort (1175–1218), often regarded as one of the founders of modern parliamentary democracy. Also included on the design is the locally ubiquitous five-petalled flower termed a cinquefoil, common amongst the civic arms of Leicestershire but rare elsewhere, and perhaps the outstanding Leicestershire motif, a fox. It has been suggested that the cinquefoil was adopted by Robert de Bellomont, 4th Earl of Leicester (d. October 1204) as a badge, in honour of his mother Pernelle or Petronilla, whose name recalls that of the flower depicted, although recent research suggests that the emblem may actually have Danish origins, being introduced to the locality by the Vikings. Both zigzag and cinquefoil, being found on civic arms across the county, are marked Leicestershire emblems, with the latter having appeared on a map of the county printed in 1784. The emblem of a fox has also been much used to represent Leicestershire, having been adopted in the nineteenth century by the county cricket team, consequently affectionately known as 'The Foxes'. A fox was subsequently included in the formal award of arms to Leicestershire County Council in 1930, in token of organised hunting in the county in the late seventeenth century, but has since become a unique Leicestershire symbol, whose modern status as a distinct county emblem now supersedes its original symbolism and reference. A fox is present on the badges and insignia of numerous Leicestershire clubs and organisations, often in combination with the cinquefoil, one example being Leicester City Football Club, also informally called 'The Foxes'. Such extended use of these symbols, often found together, made them obvious choices for deployment on the county flag. The design was promoted by a local group headed by Professor Graham Shipley of the University of Leicester, along with Sergeant Bill Brown RE of the local branch of the Royal British Legion. The flag became popular, appearing at the 2019 Glastonbury music festival and the 2021 FA Cup final and the cause was taken up by county MP Alicia Kearns who, later that year, organised a successful request for its registration by Leicestershire MPs.

Lincolnshire

Lincolnshire's colourful flag was registered on 24 October 2005. The flag was the winning entry in a competition sparked by Fred and Pat Rickett, from Moulton in the county, keen caravanners, who enquired why there was no flag that they could fly at rallies. Their plea was taken up by BBC Radio Lincolnshire, who launched the campaign in partnership with Lincolnshire Life magazine. It was supported by many local businesses, who recognised an opportunity to promote trade and tourism. This winning design, created by Michelle Andrews, features a red cross and gold Fleur de Lys, found on the civic arms of the county town, Lincoln. The alternating green and blue quadrants formed by the red cross, represent respectively, the county's agricultural heritage, and the sea off its long coastline and wide blue skies. The cross is edged in gold, a reference both to the golden crops grown in the county and the distinctive nickname 'Yellerbellies' given to people born and bred in Lincolnshire. The flag has become very popular and is widely seen flying across the county and often found on products produced in Lincolnshire.

The flag of Lincolnshire.

Middlesex

Middlesex's flag was included on the registry from its inception. In the early Anglo-Saxon era the territory of Middlesex originally formed part of the kingdom of the East Saxons. The same emblem of three gold-hilted, white Anglo-Saxon swords, termed seaxes, on a red background that represented Essex was therefore also used in Middlesex, by such bodies as militia units and county authorities. They are found, for example, on the pediment of the 'Old Middlesex Sessions House' (courthouse) in Clerkenwell, built in 1779. The three seaxes are present on Thomas Conder's eighteenth-century 'British Traveller' map of the county, and were adopted in the nineteenth century by Middlesex Cricket Club and included as a decorative feature on a pillar of Kew Bridge built in 1903 to link Middlesex and Surrey.

Having been formed in 1889, Middlesex County Council applied for distinctive arms of its own in 1910 under the direction of prominent local historian, council chairman and Deputy Lord Lieutenant Montagu Sharp. The advice of an author on military badges, Colonel Otley Parry, a Justice of the Peace for the county, was sought for a distinctive charge that would 'difference' the arms to be used by Middlesex County Council from those used by their Essex counterparts. The choice was a gold 'Saxon Crown', as appears on a silver penny from the time of King Athelstan (924–39), the earliest form of crown associated with the English monarchy. This was duly added over the three seaxes. Several examples, however, demonstrate that a crown was often included as an additional decoration alongside the seaxes, suggesting that this was a common practice that became formalised. From 1910 to 1965 the coat of arms with crown and seaxes remained the property of the Middlesex County Council as the arms holders (armigers). That body was abolished in 1965 and as there was no longer any arms holder, upon the creation of its registry, the Flag Institute took the view that the arms and an armorial banner, a flag formed from them, had effectively been released to the public. The banner was therefore included on the registry as the county flag of Middlesex and was designated as a traditional design on the basis that the essential pattern of three seaxes had been used there for centuries.

The flag of Middlesex flying in the county.

Norfolk

The flag of Norfolk was registered on 11 September 2014 as a traditional design, being a banner of the arms attributed to Ralph (Ranulph) de Gael (de Guader), 1st Earl of Norfolk (1071–75). The simple, bold design was widely known throughout the county owing to its incorporation in the arms borne by the local county council and their consequent appearance across the territory on council vehicles, sites and documentation. Deployment of the De Gael arms, which were no longer borne by an existing arms holder, as the basis for the council arms, highlighted their status as the traditional Norfolk symbol. They can be found on souvenir crockery items from the county, have been adapted by the Norfolk Heraldry Society to form its own arms and above all, were actually used as a flag by the Norfolk Broads Yacht Club as a club pennant. Recognising the widespread and long-standing usage of the design in the county, resident Dominic Victor Maverick Smith led the successful campaign to see it registered as the Norfolk flag, receiving the express support of a number of local groups and companies. It is thought that the ermine bend (the diagonal stripe from top left to bottom right) found in the design may well have been a reference to Brittany, where Ralph was Lord of Gael, and ermine is a common local emblem which also features on the Breton flag. It has been depicted

The flag of Norfolk flying in the county.

with differing realisations but for the campaign a precise form was perfected by D. V. M. Smith in consultation with the Flag Institute.

Northamptonshire

The flag of Northamptonshire was the winning entry in a competition held by the local county council and was unveiled at a ceremony held at County Hall in Northampton on 11 September 2014. This winning design was deemed to be a joint submission by two separate entrants,

Brady Ell and Ian Chadwick, who had independently contrived designs that were so similar that the judging panel declared them to be a joint submission. Brady Ells had crafted his basic design of a gold cross against a dark red background, some years previously, adding a black edging (fimbriation) to the gold cross for the competition to recall the county's leather boot and shoe industry. The dark red or maroon and gold hues found on the flag are the club colours of Northamptonshire County Cricket Club, Northamptonshire County Bowling Association, Northamptonshire Basketball Club, Northamptonshire Golf Union and Northampton Town Football Club. Evidently the definitive sporting colours of the county, this unique combination was the obvious colour scheme to assign to the county flag. At the centre of the cross sits a red rose, an emblem long used in Northamptonshire by a great many organisations. The county is affectionately known as the 'Rose of the Shires'. The link with the red rose emblem extends back to at least

Huntingdonshire, Northamptonshire and Bedfordshire at the tripoint of the three counties.

1665, when heraldic historian C. W. Scott-Giles reports, it appeared on a seal used by the county magistrates in Quarter Sessions and is believed to recall a historic association with the house of Lancaster: Elizabeth Woodville, wife of Lancastrian King Edward IV (r. 1461–83) and ancestor of every English monarch since Henry VIII and every Scottish monarch since James V, was born at Grafton Regis in the county. The competition's judging panel decided to ensure that the county would have a unique rose to avoid misidentification with the rose emblems of other counties. Consequently, a distinct Northamptonshire rose was formed through the combination of elements appearing in the various roses across the county – including a cinquefoil shape from the centre of the county council logo, the maroon or dark red colour of the county cricket club rose, the gold inner petals of the Northamptonshire Golf Union rose along with an upwards orientation of the central sepal and inclusion of two tiers of petals – resulting in the unique and attractive 'Northamptonshire rose' present on the registered flag.

Northumberland

Northumberland's flag was included on the registry from its inception. Strictly, the flag is a banner of the arms of the Northumberland County Council but its origins predate the council by more than a millennium and it is certainly part of an ancient local tradition.

The seventh-century King and Saint Oswald founded the kingdom of Northumbria by merging his domain of Bernicia with its southern neighbour Deira. The Venerable Bede, England's first historian, writing in his *Historia Ecclesiastica Gentis Anglorum*, describes Oswald's tomb where 'they hung up over the monument his banner made of gold and purple'. It is probable that this description caused the medieval heralds to assign anachronistic arms of eight alternate stripes of red and gold (yellow) to Bernicia. Before its award of arms in 1951, the Northumberland County Council had informally used these attributed stripes of Bernicia although the arms formally granted to the council by the College of Arms modified this basic design by dividing the stripes with an 'embattled' line, that is, an indentation which resembles a castle's crenelations The modification was intended to symbolise the interlocking stones of Hadrian's Wall, which runs through the county, and Northumberland's position as a border shire. Whilst the formal grant of arms meant that strictly an armorial banner formed from them would belong to and represent only Northumberland County Council, the historical references to red (purple) and gold-striped banners indicated an association of the

The Northumberland flag in a strong breeze.

territory and the pattern dating back some 1,200 years. More than just a device of the century-old council, the design was intrinsically a symbol of the over a thousand years old county. The council accordingly voted to 'release' its banner of arms for general use by Northumberland folk on 15 November 1995 and the Flag Institute duly included it as the county flag when the registry was created in the following decade. The popular design is sufficiently ingrained in the local culture to decorate bus stops and is much used, also flying at points where Northumberland shares a border with Scotland.

Nottinghamshire

Nottinghamshire's flag was the winning design in a competition organised by BBC Radio Nottingham presenter Andy Whittaker, registered on 20 May 2011. The presenter had previously successfully overseen a similar competition in neighbouring Derbyshire and as with his previous venture, the Nottinghamshire competition was initiated by suggestions from his listeners Jane Bealby and Mike Gaunt, who separately contacted the presenter asserting that the county needed a flag for the Nottinghamshire public to fly. Andy Whittaker's previous success may have encouraged the idea. The response to the suggestion was overwhelmingly positive and a panel of judges was formed, who assessed all the drawings, ideas and feedback sent to BBC Radio Nottingham to come up with the final designs. The consensus was that the flag should feature a prominent symbol of the county, the most popular being the figure of local legend Robin Hood and oak leaves. Crosses and arrows were also favoured. From a large number of submissions, the panel delivered three designs for a public vote by combining elements from the various ideas submitted.

Thousands reportedly voted in an online poll which elicited the white-edged red cross on green, bearing a green archer on a white shield as the flag of the county, a design created from ideas submitted by Richard Odams and Thomas Randall. The image of Robin Hood at the centre of England's red St George's Cross is said to mark Nottinghamshire's location at the centre of England, while the image of the archer is drawn from the outline of the statue outside Nottingham Castle, whilst the dark green background represents the county's famed green fields and forestry. The theme of Robin Hood on a shield was a popular one, with echoes of Nottinghamshire's industrial heritage, as it was used on the former logo of Home Ales, a Nottinghamshire-based firm, and a green archer, similarly facing the observer's right, was also used as its badge by Notts County Football Club between the 1950s and 1970s. The flag was raised on 24 May 2011 at ceremonies across the county.

The Nottinghamshire flag flying in the county.

Oxfordshire

Oxfordshire's flag was registered in May 2017 following a request delivered in February that year from a collection of county bodies. The design is a banner of the arms awarded in 1949 to the county council and includes the blue of Oxford University, while the white wavy stripes represent the River Thames flowing through the county. In combination with the red ox head, the arrangement of an 'ox' and a 'ford' punningly alludes to the name of the county town of 'Oxford', while the golden wheatsheaf, top right, and golden tree, bottom left, represent the agriculture and woods of the wider county which developed around it. Thus the design is a graphic expression of the name 'Ox-ford-shire'. A version of this design had been popularly and widely flown across the county and used by county organisations such as the local police, the county fire brigade, county scout troupe and various sporting teams, making it the obvious choice for registration as the county flag. The specific depiction of the elements on the registered design was fashioned by Brady Ells and Charles Ashburner.

The flag of Oxfordshire.

Rutland

The flag of England's smallest county, Rutland, was registered on 9 November 2015. The design is a banner of the arms awarded to Rutland County Council in 1950. William the Conqueror awarded land in the county to Henry de Ferrers (d. 1100), whose surname indicates a connection with iron-working or the farrier occupation.

Perhaps in recognition of this association, he claimed the 'forfeit' of a horseshoe from anyone of rank visiting his lordship in Oakham; royalty, peers of the realm and noblemen would present a horseshoe to the Castle Hall in Oakham, which now houses a large and unique collection! Oakham castle was constructed by Walchelin de Ferrers (d. 1201), great-grandson of Henry, who unsurprisingly bore arms bearing the horseshoes with which the family had become strongly associated and this symbol thus became associated with the county.

A gold horseshoe on a green shield appeared on John Speed's 1610 map of Rutland and a horseshoe is present on the 1784 'A New Map of the Counties of Leicester & Rutland, Drawn from the

The county flag on Oakham Butter Cross with All Saints' in the background, Rutland.

Latest Authorities' by Thomas Conder. By at least 1837, the colour scheme of a gold horseshoe on a green background had become fixed. By 1908 cap badges bearing a horseshoe were being worn by Rutland Police and a formal award of arms was made to Rutland County Council in 1950 with the gold horseshoe against the green field, which had become the accepted local depiction. The official description states that the green field represents the county's agriculture. Strewn across the shield are golden acorns which symbolise the extensive forest that once covered much of the county, reflected in the name of the county town, Oakham. The acorns are also deemed to represent 'smallness', an allusion to Rutland's position as England's smallest county. Since then, many county organisations, clubs and businesses have made use of the traditional Gold Horseshoe on Green to represent the county of Rutland on their insignia and labelling. Following an approach by flag enthusiast Jason Saber to A. J. Brown, the High Sheriff of Rutland, regarding registering a flag for the county, consultation with the local council led to the release of its banner of arms for use by the general public and subsequent registration.

Shropshire

The flag of Shropshire (Salop) was registered in March 2012. The flag is a banner of the arms of the local county council, which were awarded in 1895. These arms are themselves derived from the arms of the county town, Shrewsbury. While the feline heads appeared in the fifteenth century on the seal of the Corporation of Shrewsbury, their precise origin is unknown. It is speculated that they may have been fashioned from the royal arms of England, possibly in consequence of the appearance of the three lions on a charter received from Richard I in 1189. The cats' heads are colloquially known as 'loggerheads'. One theory behind this unusual term is that it refers to the practice of carving animal heads on the battering point of a log, used as a battering ram. Although based upon the arms of Shrewsbury, the county council arms are distinguished by having the leopards' faces appear on three 'piles'. These are triangular divisions of the shield, two pointing down and one up, formed by the imposition of a 'w' shape (in heraldic terminology a 'fess dancetty') in erminois, a gold pattern bearing traditional black heraldic marks indicative of fur pelts. These arms were awarded to the council on 18 June 1896, not long after its formation, and appear to have been an innovative creation of the College of Arms. With poorly rendered versions of the armorial banner becoming available, Shropshire native and artist John Yates was motivated to seek release of the banner of the council's arms to the public for registration as the county flag. He produced a more accurate depiction with correct colours, proportions and superior artistry, making the faces of the leopards bold and fierce. He secured the support of Martin Stevens, from the Lord Lieutenant's office and council legal department, whose confirmation to the Flag Institute meant that the council approved the new Yates version for use as the county flag, resulting in its subsequent registration.

Somerset

Somerset's flag was registered on 4 July 2013, the day it was announced as the winning entry in a competition organised by a county law firm and local media. Although the winner of the competition however, the design was basically traditional, having been used for the previous century by the local county council on its coat of arms and being derived from devices borne by Alfred the Great and his kinsmen. Such items were based in turn on Celtic use of a dragon symbol, which ultimately derived from the Draco device used by the military during the Roman occupation of Britain. In essence therefore, the flag has a pedigree of some 2,000 years. Originating as a windsock borne by Rome's enemies the Dacians, the legions adopted the device and bore it on their imperial ventures, including Britannia. The Romano-Britons of the fifth century retained many of the cultural imports and the significance of the Roman military emblem is suggested by references in early Welsh records to 'draig' and 'dragon', meaning warrior, and great warriors are called 'pendraig', pendragon, meaning 'dragon head'. A romanticised account by the medieval writer Geoffrey of Monmouth in his *The History of the Kings of Britain* relates that Arthur's father, Uther, is said to have seen a golden dragon in the sky upon his accession to the crown, interpreted by Merlin as an omen of success in attaining the kingship. Geoffrey writes also of Uther's successor, Arthur, who has a golden helmet carved in the shape of a 'dragon', suggesting that such devices were used as crests over a war helmet, as an emblem of leadership, the 'dragon head' mentioned. When the invading West Saxons fought against their Romano-Celtic opponents they would have become familiar with this emblem of leadership and it is likely that the West Saxons, who formed the kingdom of Wessex, adopted this emblem from them either as a symbol of their ultimate triumph over their enemy or perhaps in simple recognition of the device's intrinsic splendour.

The Anglo-Norman historian Henry of Huntingdon wrote of Cuthred of Wessex bearing a golden dragon standard at the Battle of Burford in 752 when he triumphed over the Mercians and refers to its use again in 1016, by the army of King Edmund Ironside, at the Battle of Ashingdon against Canute. Such dragon standards are also seen borne by the English army, on the Bayeux Tapestry. John Speed includes a golden dragon on a red background as the emblem of Wessex in his 1610 *Atlas of Great Britaine* and Somerset Cricket Club, in the nineteenth century, adopted a dragon for its badge, as did the West Somerset Yeomanry at the turn of the twentieth century. A red dragon on a golden background was then formally awarded to Somerset County Council in 1911. The reversal of colours may have been intended to emphasise the early association of the emblem with the Celtic inhabitants, a red dragon of course appearing on the Welsh national flag. A dragon was subsequently adopted by many and various county-based organisations and the council's emblem, often rendered as a modern logo, occasionally flew on a white cloth. In 2007, county resident Ed Woods, realising that the county had not secured a flag for itself, sought to establish the dragon as the Somerset flag. After several years his efforts initiated a county flag competition sponsored by local law firm Pardoes and Ed submitted the traditional dragon, which, with its overwhelming history and cultural legacy, won the competition.

The flag of Somerset.

The popular flag is widely flown and a dragon, as found on the county flag, carved in wood by local chainsaw artist Matthew Crabb, was revealed in Taunton High Street in 2023.

Staffordshire

The flag of Staffordshire was registered on 28 March 2016. It features the county's traditional knot emblem in gold, against a red chevron, on a gold field. Used as a badge by the local De Stafford nobility, the Stafford Knot has been associated with the county for centuries. It appears as decoration on an artifact amongst the 'Staffordshire Hoard', unearthed in the county in 2009 and estimated to date from the seventh or eighth centuries. The device can be found on old maps and has been used by military regiments, local police and county sports teams. It also appears on the civic arms of a number of county towns, was included on the seal used by the county council before being part of the arms formally received by the body in 1931 and is often found as a decorative feature across the county on various structures. A red chevron on gold are the arms of the local De Stafford nobility, present on John Speed's 1611 map of Staffordshire in combination with the gold knot and on Joan Blaeu's 1648 map. The chevron is further found on several of the civic arms across the county and is again seen in combination with the Stafford Knot on the 1931 county council arms. This traditional pattern was therefore

The flag of Staffordshire.

promoted by the Staffordshire Heritage Group in 2016, when efforts to establish a flag for the county were initiated. This simple design was voted as the winner in a contest with the armorial banner of the county council, a similar but more detailed arrangement.

Suffolk

Suffolk's flag was added to the registry on 9 October 2017. The design is the armorial banner of the arms attributed to Saint Edmund, a golden crown 'pierced' by two golden arrows, against a blue background. The banner is understood to have flown in July 1954 to welcome Princess Margaret to the Suffolk Regiment following her appointment as its colonel in chief. It was raised again in 2017, on 21 June, the inaugural Suffolk Day, by Suffolk County Council and consequently registered as the county flag with the support of some twenty-one county organisations. The emblem of crown and crossed arrows reflects Saint Edmund's kingship of East Anglia and the manner of his death, in a shower of Viking arrows. It is found across the county in civic arms, company logos and the badges of county-based organisations and clubs and in varying depictions the combination of gold arrows and crown on blue has also often appeared on maps of the county. This much-used, acknowledged county emblem, with its long-standing local heritage, was therefore the natural choice for registration as the county's flag and is promoted by county native and enthusiast for all things Suffolk, Ben Archer.

Surrey

The Surrey flag was registered as a traditional design on 11 September 2014. The flag is a banner of the arms used by the family of William de Warenne, 1st Earl of Surrey, which has enjoyed a long association with the county since its first reference in the thirteenth-century 'Glover's Roll' of arms and subsequent mention in the seventeenth-century poem by Michael Drayton on the Battle of Agincourt, where he wrote, 'The men of Surrey, checky blue and gold, which for brave Warenne their first earl they wore.' The straightforward checkered pattern reflects its antiquity, originating when the notion of identification of armoured individuals by distinct patterns and colours first took hold, with initially bold, simple arrangements. These gradually became more complex as the practice became widespread and greater distinction was required for larger numbers. Whilst the family line that bore these checks died out in the seventeenth century, the pattern has since been repeatedly used by various Surrey organisations across the years, including the county's archaeological society in the nineteenth century and a number of sporting bodies, and has been incorporated into the civic arms of several Surrey towns. A number of councils across the county raised the De Warenne banner in 2014 on the inaugural County Flags Day which led to its registration as the county flag. In recent years, thanks to the efforts of county native Neil Thompson the flag has flown widely, especially on the county day, each May.

Sussex

Sussex's flag of six gold martlets, essentially a heraldic representation of a swallow, on a blue background appeared as a county emblem in John Speed's 1611 *Atlas of Great Britaine*, representing the kingdom of the South Saxons. The arms of families of great repute or status have often become strongly associated with the counties where they reside and it is likely that Sussex's martlets arose in like manner as the personal arms of a man of local importance. Available historical sources indicate that this was most likely the fourteenth-century Knight of the Shire Sir John de Radynden, who bore arms of silver martlets on a blue shield. He sat in Parliament, organised the lighting of signal beacons and deployment of watchmen and campaigned in

France, providing 140 armed Sussex footmen and 400 archers. With the troops he mustered for battle gathering under his coat of arms, there was likely to have been a well-developed association of the de Radynden insignia and the county where he was so influential, and it is speculated that his arms appearing on documents relating to county affairs were retained by his successors as a mark of office. This theory is presented on a plaque in Preston Park in the county, now a public space, marking the site of Radynden Manor, which includes the advice 'ABOVE ARE THE ARMS OF SIR JOHN DE RADYNDEN 1274 – 1350 SINCE ASSUMED BY THE COUNTY OF SUSSEX'. The martlets were adopted in 1846 by the Sussex Archaeological Society and by Sussex Cricket Club in the early nineteenth century and have since been embraced by a great number of clubs and organisations in the county. Their deployment as the county flag of Sussex was the result of a campaign by residents Dave and Brady Ells, whose extensive research led to their registration as the county flag of Sussex on 20 May 2011. The popular flag is today widely flown across the county.

The county flag in Eastbourne, Sussex.

Warwickshire

The Warwickshire flag was registered on 15 August 2016. The flag is a modern reworking of the county's traditional county emblem of a white bear and ragged staff on a red background. The precise origins of the bear and ragged staff emblem are lost to the distant past and are the subject of legend but have been associated with the Earls of Warwick since at least the fourteenth century. Since this time they have been frequently used, both separately and in combination, as decorative features on a wide variety of objects and heraldically, as badges, on seals and as a crest, over the shield, in the coat of arms borne by the Earl. The combined bear and ragged staff emblem is found on John Speed's 1611 map of the county of Warwickshire, in his *Atlas of Great Britaine* and was worn as a collar badge by the 1st Warwickshire Militia regiment, originally raised in 1759. They have since become generally associated with the county and used for the badges and insignia of numerous county organisations and sporting bodies, including the county council, the local police force and the county cricket club. Such widespread use and recognition made the emblem the obvious choice for deployment as the county flag and a version was fashioned that avoided infringing depictions on existing arms, as dictated by strict heraldic rules, which was supported by the county's Lord Lieutenant, Tim Cox, and High Sheriff, Richard Samuda, and duly registered.

The flag of Warwickshire.

Westmorland

Westmorland's flag was registered on 30 September 2011. The choice of design was a banner of arms of the former county council of Westmorland, felt to be most appropriate because of its local familiarity on plaques, pictures, vehicles and badges and its continued use by the county football association. The arms from which the flag derives were awarded to the former county council in 1926 and combine two red bars on a white background, which were taken from the arms of the de Lancaster family, who were Barons of Kendal, with a heraldically stylised gold apple tree from the thirteenth-century seal of the borough of Appleby, the county town. The popular flag's registration was supported by a number of county organisations.

Wiltshire

Wiltshire's flag was registered on 1 December 2009 following a declaration of support for the design by the Wiltshire County Council. The flag is the creation of county resident Mike Prior and his daughter Helen Pocock. It features a Great Bustard (Otis tarda) at its centre, a bird native to the county which had been extinct since 1832 but was recently returned as part of an intensive ten-year breeding programme on Salisbury Plain. The design is inspired by the coat of arms awarded to Wiltshire County Council in 1937, which features a great bustard as the crest over the shield and a pattern of green and white stripes recalling the county's pasturelands and chalk downs, which in the flag bend to the centre from both vertical edges to represent the undulating green downs of the county over their chalk underlay.

The bustard is depicted in a gold hue against a solid green circle, to illustrate the open grassland where it lives. Surrounding the circle are six alternate green and white 'sections' intended to convey both the county's famed ancient stone circles at Stonehenge and Avebury (each 'section' representing a rock) and in an abstract fashion the county itself, which is surrounded by six neighbours, namely (clockwise) Gloucestershire, Oxfordshire, Berkshire, Hampshire, Dorset and Somerset – albeit that Oxfordshire and Wiltshire do not actually touch. The flag's registration followed a campaign led by Mike Prior who organised its first raising on 24 September 2006, attended by the Trowbridge town crier in full regalia. The flag was raised by Lord Bath and Mayor of Trowbridge Tom James. Three years later the Great Bustard flag was formally approved by the council during a full meeting and duly registered as the county flag of Wiltshire.

Worcestershire

The flag of Worcestershire was registered on 8 April 2013 when it was raised over Worcestershire Cathedral and revealed as the winner of a county flag competition held by BBC Hereford and Worcester. It was designed by county resident Elaine Truby and was one of four designs selected from the entries submitted by a judging panel for a public vote, which it won. The flag features three of the county's famed black pears, a symbol which the seventeenth-century poet Michael Drayton in his poem on the Battle of Agincourt, asserted was the emblem borne by men from the county, 'Wor'ster a pear tree laden with its fruit'. A further legend holds that the Worcester Archers rallied under pear trees before the battle and pear blossom was borne as a badge by the Worcestershire Yeomanry Cavalry from the beginning of the twentieth century until 1956. The fruit's dull, purplish skin gives it a black appearance, hence the name. Three of these pears are seen on a shield, which sits against a wavy green and blue background. These latter colours symbolise the verdant flood plain of the River Severn as it runs through the county. The trio of pears draws upon a pattern found on the civic arms of the county town of Worcester and repeated on the badges of the county cricket club, the local police force and Worcester rugby club.

Yorkshire

The flag of Yorkshire was registered in 2008. It bears a white rose which may have originated with the first Duke of York, Edmund of Langley, in the fourteenth century, who founded the House of York as a cadet branch of the then ruling House of Plantagenet. An alternative view holds that the rose was a badge of the Mortimer family, whose member Anne married Edmund's younger son Richard. Their son, also Richard, 3rd Duke of York and father of Edward IV, claimed the throne through his Mortimer descent and therefore naturally displayed their white rose in opposition to the Lancastrian Henry VI, who bore a red rose. Tradition holds that at the Battle of Minden on 1 August 1759, Yorkshiremen of the 51st Regiment of Foot picked white roses from bushes near to the battlefields and wore them on their clothing. This act is variously described as a tribute to fallen comrades after the battle or a show of bravado. There is actually no firm account of the event, but it has certainly inspired a trenchant mythology that may have helped to develop the association of the white rose with the county and the adoption of 1 August as the county day. In the Victorian era, a crop of rose motifs appeared on the buildings of York and the following century saw white roses feature on most civic arms awarded in the county, including those of the local councils established in 1889, to administer the three Yorkshire Ridings. A white rose on blue was the regimental badge of 'The Queen's Own Yorkshire Dragoons' despatched to serve in the Second Boer War in 1899 and Yorkshire County Cricket Club also adopted a white flower device on blue for its badge, subsequently flown as a flag during matches. This colour choice may have been influenced by an eighteenth-century illustration of the Battle of Bosworth, found in William Henry Montague's *History of England* published in London *c.* 1780, which depicts the aftermath of the Battle of Bosworth, where a blue flag with a white rose is used by Yorkist forces. This popular design was increasingly raised across the county and promoted by the Yorkshire Ridings Society, which successfully sought its registration.

SCOTLAND

From left to right, flags of Scottish counties Kirkcudbrightshire, Shetland, Caithness and Orkney.

Aberdeenshire

Aberdeenshire's flag was unfurled by the county's Lord Lieutenant, Sandy Manson, at 10.30 a.m. on 22 April 2023, at a ceremony held at Castle Fraser in the county. The winning design in a competition, it depicts a white castle, both to represent Aberdeenshire as Scotland's 'Castle Country' and Balmoral Castle specifically, whose royal association is also referenced by the inclusion of a crown, a device much used in local heraldry. The castle appears against an unusual bi-coloured background of a golden-orange colour at the hoist (left) side and a purple fly (right side). The golden hue signifies both barley, reflecting the county's arable land, and the whisky which it yields, whilst the purple symbolises the heather on the mountains. The county flag was created from ideas received from pupils at Newtonhill Primary School near Stonehaven and Elrick Primary School, Westhill, and was one of four selected by a judging panel from entries received for inclusion in a public vote to decide the county flag.

Banffshire

The Banffshire flag was created by Ellie Stewart, a pupil from Portessie Primary School in the county. The winning entry in a competition, the flag was unfurled at a ceremony held at 11 o'clock on 28 October 2023, at Castle Hill, Cullen, with subsequent raisings at several other county locations. The design was one of four selected by a judging panel from entries received for inclusion in a public vote to decide the county flag. The central white band on the flag represents the arched stone bridges typical of the county, which is crossed with rivers, represented by the blue base that also recalls the county's coast. The upper orange colour, along with the symbol of a blazing sun, together symbolise Banffshire's natural sunsets and its agriculture. Below the white band, the series of orange semi-circles recalls the top view of barrels of the whisky made from the county's waters, the orange hue symbolising the amber liquid itself.

Berwickshire

The Berwickshire flag was officially registered by the Lord Lyon, Scotland's heraldic authority, on 16 November 2023. The winner in a competition organised by the Berwickshire Civic Society, which ran through June of the same year, the flag was one of five finalists selected by a judging panel for inclusion in a public vote, held through October, with this winning design receiving over half of the votes cast.

Between an upper blue panel and a lower green one, the central chain represents the Union Chain Bridge, which spans the River Tweed between Horncliffe in Northumberland and Fishwick in the county, which symbolises the historic fluctuations of the Anglo-Scottish border and Berwickshire's important role as a link between the two nations. The salmon against the blue background reflects both the importance of the local maritime fishing industry and the county's recreational fishing activity and is also a nod to the Berwickshire Marine Reserve, an area off the county's coast designated to protect marine biodiversity and to promote responsible recreational use and sustainable fishing. The golden ear of barley, against the green base, represents the county's agriculture. The respective colours thus recall the sea and the land.

Caithness

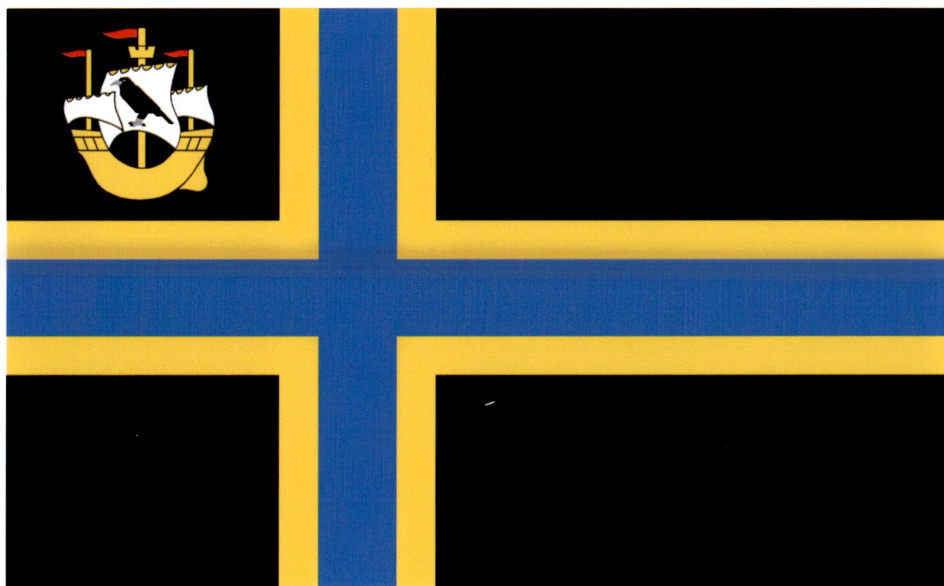

The flag of Caithness was unfurled on 26 January 2016 at a ceremony held at New Caithness House, Wick. The winner of a competition, the design features a Nordic cross – that is, one offset to the left – symbolising the ancient ties of the county to the Vikings. The black base colour of the flag recalls the area's famous Caithness flagstone, whilst the gold and blue refer to its beaches and the sea. The galley in the canton is considered the traditional emblem of the county; it bears a raven on its sail, an acknowledged Viking symbol which had appeared in the arms borne by the former Caithness County Council. Inspired by the flags adopted by nearby Orkney and Shetland, like Caithness possessed of a marked Scandinavian heritage, the notion of a flag for the county had been under consideration for several years. Local media and local authorities subsequently worked together to organise the competition in March 2015, which elicited 327 entries, from which a judging panel selected four finalists for a public vote. This winning design received over 40 per cent of the votes cast and Caithness duly became the first mainland Scottish county to fly its own flag.

East Lothian

The East Lothian flag was revealed on 13 December 2018 and created by local man Archie Martin, a landscape architect at East Lothian Council. The design won a public vote of four competing finalists, selected by a panel, as the final stage of a competition launched in late November 2017 by the county council in cooperation with several other bodies. The competition closed on 28 February 2018, having received 623 entries from across the globe. The voided gold diagonal cross or saltire, on blue, recalls the tradition that Athelstaneford in the county is the birthplace of the national flag of Scotland, Saint Andrew's Cross. The blue stripes through the gold are also intended to represent the county's rivers, Esk and Tyne, with the gold colour signifying the wealth of East Lothian's farmlands and reputation as the granary of Scotland and recalling the traditional sun symbol of the Lothian region, as one theory holds that the name Lothian may derive from the name of the Celtic god of light, 'Lugus'. The lion rampant is taken from the arms of the East Lothian Council and found on the arms of local nobility such as the Earl of Dunbar.

Kirkcudbrightshire

The flag of Kirkcudbrightshire was registered as the result of consultation by the county's Lord Lieutenant, Sir Malcolm Ross, from late 2015, with the Flag Institute's Philip Tibbetts who created the flag. The design was embraced by the county official, who subsequently petitioned Scotland's heraldic authority, the Lord Lyon, for its registration. It was formally unveiled on Saturday 11 June and duly added to the registry. The county town of Kirkcudbright was named for Saint Cuthbert, whose remains were kept there for seven years. A pectoral cross was found on the saint's body when his tomb was opened in the nineteenth century and this is the style of cross featured on the flag. The former county council used arms which featured a chequered band of green and white to recall the checked tablecloth used by local stewards when collecting taxes. The colours of the flag are accordingly the distinct green and white of the 'Stewartry of Kirkcudbright', counter-changed to reflect those green and white checks.

Moray

The Moray flag was the winning design in a competition held in 2023. It was created by Aila Gibson from Dallas Primary School in the county and revealed at a ceremony held at Elgin Town Hall on 28 October 2023, with the county's Lord Lieutenant, Seymour Monro. The flag's green hoist and golden garb, or wheatsheaf, recall the rich agricultural output of the county. A gold band over blue, divided by a wavy partition, together represent the sand and sea of the county's coast. This reference further alludes to the origin of the name Moray itself, coming from Gaelic or Pictish terms indicating a marine connection. A wheatsheaf had featured on a seal used by the former Moray County Council, for its documentation, where it appeared on a shield supported by two lions, from 1890 until the body was officially awarded a coat of arms on 20 July 1927. The choice of a garb was itself inspired by its earlier appearance on the seal used by the seventeenth-century 'Commisariat of Moray', an administrative body that comprised territory across the region.

Orkney

For some years, residents in Orkney had flown a yellow flag bearing an offset red cross, in typical Scandinavian form, to reflect the archipelago's heritage. Scotland's heraldic authority, the Lord Lyon, refused to register the popular design for being too similar to existing arms, necessitating a competition to find a distinct flag for the island county. The winning flag, which topped an island-wide vote of five finalists with 53 per cent and also featuring a Scandinavian-type cross, was created by Duncan Tullock, a postman from Birsay, and registered on 10 April 2007. From around 100 submissions, a judging panel selected an initial twelve which were then reduced to the final five. The colours red and yellow, both found on the royal banners of Norway and Scotland, are combined with the blue of the sea which surrounds Orkney and which is also the principal colour of Scotland's national flag, Saint Andrew's Cross. The Orkney flag is much used by county sports teams and has been adapted for its kit by the county's Island Games team.

Shetland

Shetland and its sister archipelago of Orkney share a status more akin to an assimilated territory than a straightforward county and in spite of over 500 years of Scottish and British rule, their culture remains eminently Scandinavian. This is reflected in the form of the Shetland flag, an offset cross typical of all the Scandinavian or Nordic nations, rendered in the blue and white colours of Scotland's Saint Andrew's Cross, which neatly encapsulates the islands' mingled heritage and history. The flag was designed by students Roy Grønneberg and Bill Adams in 1969 to commemorate the 500th anniversary of the transfer of the islands from Norway to the Kingdom of Scotland and the 500 years before the transfer, as part of Norway. In 1985 a representative from Shetland's tourist office, Maurice Mullay, visiting Sweden as part of a promotional campaign, was asked if Shetland had a special regional flag and recalled the Grønneberg/ Adams design with its Scandinavian association, which immediately appealed to his Swedish hosts. Consequently two Swedish yachts visiting Lerwick bore the blue and white 'Shetland' cross from their mastheads as a courtesy.

Shetland's participation in the 1985 Island Games on the Isle of Man was marked by the appearance of the flag there. Additionally, the Shetland tourist office included the flag on its tourist literature and sold thousands of actual flags to both locals and visitors. It began to appear on boats, cars and outside hotels. Although unofficial, the flag had become popular and was gradually accepted as the islands' flag. In 2005 the heraldic authority in Scotland, the Lord Lyon, made an official grant of the flag to the local council. This official recognition came in time for the 2005 Island Games and the flag was officially adopted with a description by the Shetland Islands Council (SIC) on 13 December 2006. The flag is regularly flown, is much used by county sports teams and is often found on vessels and aircraft.

Sutherland

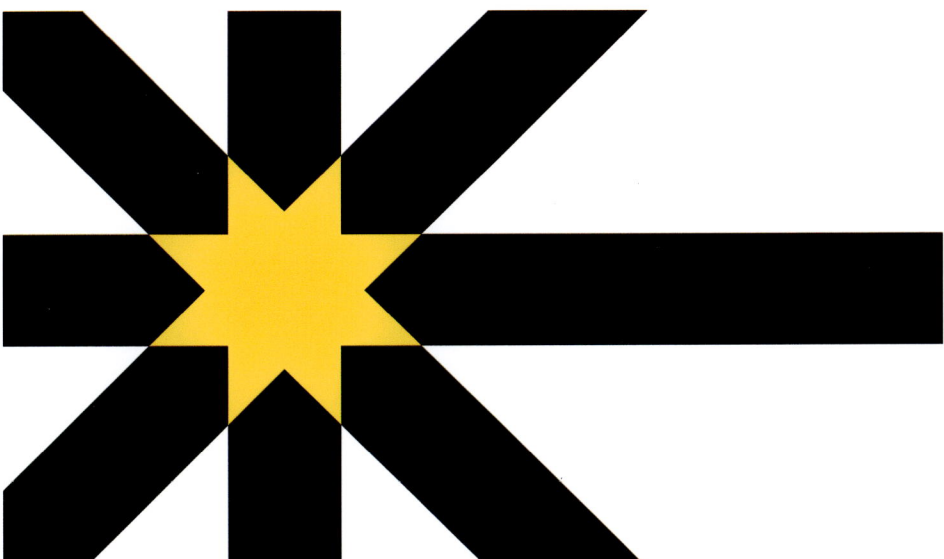

Sutherland's flag was registered on 14 December 2018. It was the winner in a vote of four options held in November 2018; the designer was not announced. The combined saltire and Nordic cross denotes Sutherland's early history as a Scottish territory under Viking control. At the point where the arms of the two crosses meet is a golden sun, which is said to symbolise the sun raised high in the south for the origin of the county name 'South Land' as well as the sunrises seen on the east coast and the sunsets on the county's west coast. The black colour of the cross recalls the peat of the 'flow country' and dark skies and together with the white background, recall the central colours of the coat of arms of the former Sutherland council, which depicted a black raven or eagle against a white field. The vote that led to this flag had been arranged following plangent criticism of the original selection process and the design that it elicited in a competition to secure a flag for the county. The chosen design was a red and gold bi-colour, against which was a front-facing swooping eagle that was divided gold against a red background and red against a gold background, with three gold stars along the hoist (left side), with the specific depiction of the eagle itself also heavily criticised. Both eagle and stars were common features on local arms and insignia in the county. This originally chosen flag had been fashioned by the judging panel – which included a number of children from local schools – from elements found in several of the competition entries.

WALES

Anglesey

The flag of Anglesey/Ynys Môn was registered on 7 March 2014 following a request by the Ymgyrch Baner Sir Fôn (Anglesey Flag Campaign), headed by island native Gwyndaf Parri, who had previously been successful in securing a flag for the neighbouring county of Caernarfonshire. Originating as the arms attributed to the locally celebrated ruler, Hwfa ap Cynddlw, the design of three gold lions and a gold chevron on a red background, subsequently used by a number of local bodies including the local police, fire brigade and adapted by the county council, had an evident long-standing association with the island county, making it the natural choice to be the island's flag.

The flag of Anglesey flying in the county.

Caernarfonshire

The flag of Caernarfonshire was registered in March 2012. The arrangement of three golden eagles on a green field originates with their attribution as the arms of the twelfth-century king Owain Gwynedd, of the erstwhile kingdom of Gwynedd. The heart of Caernarfonshire, around Mount Snowdon, is known in Welsh as 'Eryri', meaning 'land or nest of eagles', so the association is an obvious one. Additionally, Segontium Fort, constructed by the Romans in AD 77, was located in modern-day Caernarfon town, fuelling speculation that typical Roman usage of eagle symbols may have influenced their presence in local heraldry. Three eagles were also found on the 'Eagle Tower' of Caernarfon Castle, completed in 1284, whose three turrets were each topped by a stone eagle. The definite link between the county and the trio of raptors was well forged by the seventeenth century when they appeared on John Speed's 1610 map of Caernarfonshire. Poet Michael Drayton wrote of troops from the county in his celebrated 1627 poem 'Battle of Agincourt', 'Those of Caernarfon not the least in speed…Three golden Eagles in their Ensigne brought'. The emblem has subsequently been widely deployed in the insignia of local organisations and clubs and in light of their extensive use and long historical association, it was felt that that there could be no more appropriate design for registration as the Caernarfonshire flag. This was sought by local resident Gwyndaf Pari who led the successful campaign.

Flintshire

The flag of Flintshire/Sir Y Fflint was registered on 25 February 2015. The design is a traditional county emblem, first attributed to the local eleventh-century ruler, Edwin of Tegeingl, a Welsh 'cantref' and sometime kingdom that covered much of the territory of

Flintshire. The design features a black cross on a white field, between four choughs, a bird which once flourished on the limestone range which runs along part of Flintshire's coast. The distinctive form of the cross is described heraldically as 'engrailed' and 'flory', referring respectively to its scalloped edging and the flower-like decorations at the ends of the cross's arms. The successful campaign to see this design, which had been much used across the years by various sporting bodies and cultural associations in the county, registered as the flag of Flintshire, was organised by the Grŵp Cefnogwyr Baner Sir Fflint/Flintshire Flag Supporters Group, headed by Dr Shaun Evans, and enjoyed extensive local support from over two dozen Flintshire-based organisations and a number of individual politicians and councillors.

Glamorgan

Glamorgan's flag is a banner of the arms attributed to Iestyn Ap Gwrgant (1045–93), the last native ruler of the kingdom of Morgannwg, on which Glamorgan is based. The design of three white chevronels (small chevrons) on a red background is prevalent on the civic heraldry of councils across Glamorgan and is frequently found on historical records and amongst military insignia linked with the

Monmouthshire and Glamorgan flags at the Rhymney river county boundary.

county. The flag was registered on 24 September 2013, at the request of the Glamorgan History Society, supported by a number of other cultural and historical associations in the county.

Merioneth

The unusual and rather striking flag of Merioneth (Meirionydd/ Merionethshire) was registered on 2 January 2015 as a traditional design. It is an adaptation of the seal used by the former

Merionethshire County Council, which in turn derived from the description of a banner borne by the men of the county at the Battle of Agincourt in the seventeenth-century poem of the same name by Michael Drayton. Here he wrote of 'three goats dancing 'gainst a rising sun' – the shield was blue, the sun golden and the goats white. Speculation regarding this unusual arrangement suggests a connection with Cader Idris, where goats browsed and behind which the sun rose. The same design had appeared on decorative plates and chinaware as souvenir items from the county and been adapted as a badge by a county club, Clwb Rhedeg Meirionnydd (Merioneth Running Club), who successfully requested its registration. The county flag maintains a theme associated with Merioneth for several centuries and is highly distinctive; no other British flag is similar.

Monmouthshire

Monmouthshire's flag was registered on 30 September 2011 following a resolution of support by Monmouthshire County Council. The design originates with the arms attributed by medieval heralds to the sixth-century king, Inyr, of the Kingdom of Gwent, the forerunner to Monmouthshire, although no information has yet come to light detailing the significance of this particular arrangement of three fleur de lis and the colours blue and black. The same design formed the basis of the arms now used by the Diocese of Monmouth, of the Church of Wales, and it has since been further incorporated into the arms and badges of other local bodies over the succeeding years, including Blaenau Gwent Council and Monmouthshire County Rugby Football Club. In 1948 the attributed arms of ancient Gwent were subsumed in the coat of arms awarded to Monmouthshire County Council. On the basis of this long association and general usage, flag enthusiast Jason Saber contacted his fellow Association of British Counties member Owain Vaughan regarding a proposed flag for the county and was met with a positive response. The design proposed was formed from the council arms following research into their derivation and origin. The proposed flag was thus a vertical bi-colour of a lighter shade of blue and black with three gold fleur de lis. The Monmouthshire Association was formed and in December 2010 began to promote the newly devised but anciently sourced flag which was displayed by the Monmouthshire Mounted Games Team at the June–July 2011

The flag of Monmouthshire unfurled at Glastonbury music festival.

Glanusk Horse Trials in neighbouring Brecknockshire and in July that year the flag was raised in the village of Devauden. On the back of these two instances of local usage of the flag the county council announced their official seal of approval of the design and it was duly registered.

Pembrokeshire

Pembrokeshire's flag was registered in 2008 but originally conceived in 1974 by local councillors Peter Stock, Dewi Pritchard, Jim Brock and Marjorie Jacobs in the midst of a local government Act that removed the administrative status of the county. The flag was defiantly designed and raised to announce that the county still very much existed irrespective of whatever administrative arrangements the government might impose. Its popularity grew over the decades and it was duly registered on the basis of popular use, appeal and recognition. The design of the flag is based on the flag of Saint David, a gold cross on black background, alluding to the saint's birthplace, the city of Saint David's in the county. The blue is held to represent the water of this sea girt county and the yellow of its summer sunshine. The central device is a green pentagon which

The flag of Pembrokeshire.

symbolises the green fields and clifftops of Pembrokeshire. This bears a Tudor rose as used by King Henry VII (1457–1509), born at Pembroke Castle. The Tudor rose is occasionally depicted in a quartered red and white form, although there appears to be no specific reason for this colouring on the flag. Perhaps this version is considered closer to the original Henry VII emblem? A dedication ceremony for the flag was held at Pembroke Castle on 28 July 1988, making it the official flag of the county. The ceremony included a marching display by the Queen's Dragoon Guards who performed music titled 'The Pembrokeshire Flag' written by Joffre Swales, founder and conductor of the Haverfordwest Town Band located in the county. The flag has been taken up with enthusiasm by the county's inhabitants, regularly flies from Pembroke Castle and has been adapted by local companies and organisations.